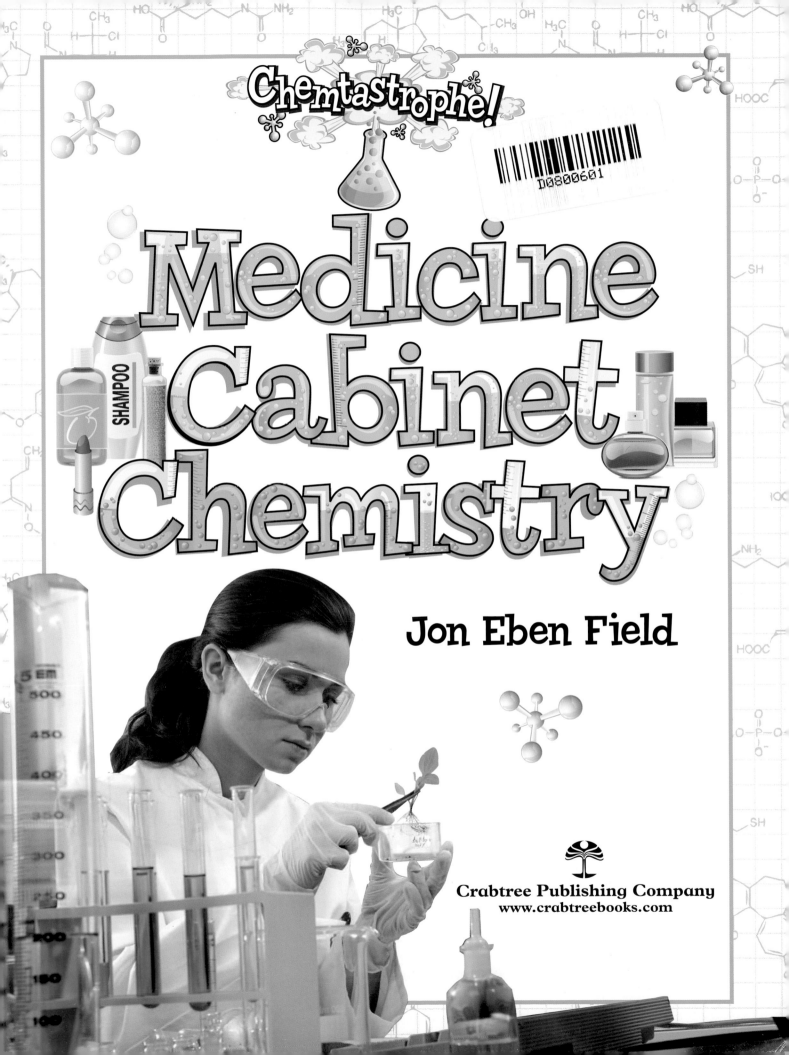

Chemtastrophe!

Medicine Cabinet Chemistry

Jon Eben Field

Crabtree Publishing Company
www.crabtreebooks.com

Crabtree Publishing Company
www.crabtreebooks.com

Photographs: Title page: Alexander Raths/Shutterstock Inc.; p.2 : Pierre Lamy Petit, French/Wikimedia Commons; p. 3: Teacept/ Shutterstock Inc.; p. 4: Petro Feketa/Shutterstock Inc.; p. 5: (bottom) Rob Byron/ Shutterstock Inc., (top) micro10x/ Shutterstock Inc.; p. 6: (bottom) Paul Cowan/ Shutterstock Inc., (top) Steve Cukrov/ Shutterstock Inc.; p. 7: (top) Roxana Bashyrova/Shutterstock Inc., (bottom) Pierre Lamy Petit, French/ Wikimedia Commons; p. 8: Laurence Gough/Shutterstock Inc.; p. 9: Rob Marmion/Shutterstock Inc.; p. 10: Laurence Gough/ Shutterstock Inc.; p. 11 (top) Laurence Gough/Shutterstock Inc., (bottom) Pierre Lamy Petit, French/Wikimedia Commons; p. 12: Lasse Kristensen/Shutterstock Inc.; p. 13: (bottom) Rob Byron/ Shutterstock Inc., (top) Graça Victoria/ Shutterstock Inc.; p. 14: Rob Byron/Shutterstock Inc.; p. 15: (top) Chris Lenfert/ Shutterstock Inc., (bottom) Felix Mizioznikov/ Shutterstock Inc.; p. 16: (top) Svetlana Lukienko/Shutterstock Inc., (bottom) Pierre Lamy Petit, French/Wikimedia Commons; p. 17: Fotocrisis/ Shutterstock Inc.; p. 18: Picsfive/Shutterstock Inc.; p. 19: Chuck Rausin/Shutterstock Inc.; p. 20-23: Jim Chernishenko; p. 24: Blinow61/Shutterstock Inc.; p. 25: (top) Olga Chirkova/ Shutterstock Inc., (middle) Carolina K. Smith, M.D./ Shutterstock Inc., (bottom) Pierre Lamy Petit, French/Wikimedia Commons; p. 26: (top) Libby Chapman/ iStockPhoto.com/ Shutterstock Inc., (bottom) Henrik Larsson/Shutterstock Inc.; p. 27: (top) Serial Coder/ Shutterstock Inc., (middle) Mike Rogal/ Shutterstock Inc., (bottom) Pierre Lamy Petit, French/Wikimedia Commons; p. 28: (left) Arvind Balaraman/ Shutterstock Inc., (right) Four Oaks/ Shutterstock Inc.; p. 29: Hywit Dimyadi/ Shutterstock Inc.; p. 30-31: Teacept/Shutterstock Inc.

Publishing plan research and development:

Sean Charlebois, Reagan Miller
Crabtree Publishing Company

Developed and Produced by: Plan B Book Packagers

Editorial director: Ellen Rodger

Art director: Rosie Gowsell-Pattison

Glossary and index: David Pula

Project coordinator: Kathy Middleton

Editor: Adrianna Morganelli

Proofreader: Crystal Sikkens

Prepress technician: Katherine Berti

Print and production coordinator: Katherine Berti

Special thanks to experimenter Nico

"How we know" boxes feature an image of 19th century French chemist and microbiologist Louis Pasteur. Famous for his groundbreaking work in the cause and prevention of diseases, his most famous discovery bears his name—pasteurization, a heating and cooling method that prevents liquids, such as milk, from passing on disease.

Library and Archives Canada Cataloguing in Publication

Field, Jon Eben, 1975-
    Medicine cabinet chemistry / Jon Eben Field.

(Chemtastrophe!)
Includes index.
Issued also in electronic format.
ISBN 978-0-7787-5287-5 (bound).--ISBN 978-0-7787-5304-9 (pbk.)

    1. Pharmaceutical chemistry--Juvenile literature.
2. Chemistry--Experiments--Juvenile literature.
I. Title. II. Series: Chemtastrophe!

RS403.F53 2011   j615'.19   C2010-906584-0

Library of Congress Cataloging-in-Publication Data

Field, Jon Eben.
 Medicine cabinet chemistry / Jon Eben Field.
    p. cm. -- (Chemtastrophe!)
 Includes index.
 ISBN 978-0-7787-5304-9 (pbk. : alk. paper) -- ISBN 978-0-7787-5287-5 (reinforced library binding : alk. paper) -- ISBN 978-1-4271-9612-5 (electronic pdf.)
 1. Pharmaceutical chemistry--Juvenile literature. 2. Aspirin--Juvenile literature. 3. Chemistry--Experiments--Juvenile literature. I. Title. II. Series.

 RS403.F54 2011
 615'.19--dc22
                         2010042066

Crabtree Publishing Company

www.crabtreebooks.com   1-800-387-7650

Printed in China/012011/GW20101014

Published in Canada
Crabtree Publishing
616 Welland Ave.
St. Catharines, ON
L2M 5V6

Published in the United States
Crabtree Publishing
PMB 59051
350 Fifth Avenue, 59th Floor
New York, New York 10118

Published in the United Kingdom
Crabtree Publishing
Maritime House
Basin Road North, Hove
BN41 1WR

Published in Australia
Crabtree Publishing
386 Mt. Alexander Rd.
Ascot Vale (Melbourne)
VIC 3032

Contents

Science and Discovery

Have you ever wondered how aspirin works? Or toothpaste? Or deodorant? Your bathroom medicine cabinet is full of substances created through the science of chemistry.

What is Science?

Science is used to explore the world, create technology, and manufacture many familiar products from shaving cream to cough syrup and hair dryers. Chemistry is a field of science that focuses mostly on matter. Matter is in everything that is around you. For example, your toothbrush is matter, the light bulbs in your bathroom are matter, and even the mirror on the medicine cabinet reflecting your face is matter. The **properties** of matter determine the hows and whys of a substance.

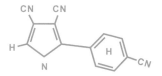

Cha...Cha...Changes

In chemistry, there are two primary kinds of change: physical and chemical. A physical change occurs when water **condenses** on the mirror after a shower. In this case, a gas is becoming a liquid. Many chemical changes occur as you brush your teeth with toothpaste. Chemistry is apparent in the **fluoride** in your toothpaste, in how soap works when you wash your hands, and in how medications work. Almost all science involves chemistry in one way or another.

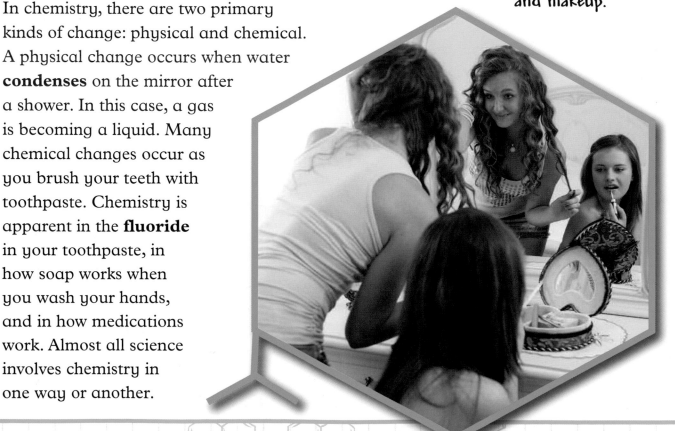

Matter is everything including mirrors and makeup.

4

Scientific Serendipity

Scientific research and advancements are responsible for many dramatic changes in the world around us. These discoveries often result from years of hard work and careful analysis. Occasionally, though, there are scientific discoveries that are considered a "lucky accident." These accidents are called serendipity. Serendipity occurs in an experiment when a scientist sees something happen that is unexpected but still very useful.

Bathroom Chemistry

Chemistry exists everywhere in the world. So, it makes sense that the bathroom in your house is full of chemistry. The electricity that powers the lights in the bathroom or the hair dryer is **conducted** on wires made of specific metals. Razor blades are extremely thin because of the properties of the metals used to make them. These metals are chemicals known as alloys. A bottle of Tylenol or Aspirin contains analgesics, or painkillers, made from chemical **compounds** that affect your nervous system when swallowed. Many lotions and creams are made from compounds discovered by chemists. Everywhere you turn in the bathroom, chemistry abounds.

Most pills and ointments in a medicine cabinet are chemical mixtures called compounds.

In the United States, medical drugs are regulated by the Food and Drug Administration (FDA). New drugs often require up to seven years of testing and trials to gain FDA approval for sale to the public.

What Matters is Matter

Matter is the substance that makes up the objects in the world around us. The water you drink is matter. Medicine cabinets, pill bottles, and nail polish are all matter.

Matter and Atoms

The idea of atoms was first proposed in ancient Greece over 2,500 years ago but was not proven until thousands of years later. The word atom meant something that could not be divided further. Atoms are too small to see with the naked eye. Using powerful microscopes, scientists have shown that atoms are made up of a dense **nucleus**.

Matter Molecules

When atoms bond together, they form more complex structures called molecules. Sometimes, molecules are made up of two of the same atom, such as oxygen (the gas we breathe), or O_2. Other molecules are made up of two different atoms, such as carbon dioxide (the gas we breathe out), or CO_2. Some other molecules are large and complicated like acetaminophen, an ingredient in many pain relievers, which has the chemical composition $C_8H_9NO_2$.

Nail polish is liquid that changes its state when dried.

States of Matter

Matter occurs in different states or forms, depending on things such as temperature, air pressure, or the amount of space available for it. Matter can be a solid, liquid, or gas. A solid is a group of atoms or molecules that are hard to the touch. Although the atoms in a solid vibrate, they are very close together and feel stable. A mirror or a toothbrush are examples of solids. Water exists as a solid when it is ice. While it is frozen solid, an ice cube will maintain its shape. As the ice melts, the water molecules become fluid and move around more freely. If boiled, water's molecules spread out very quickly and some escape as steam. Even though water can be a solid, liquid, or gas, these changes in state are only physical changes. All of the changes are reversible and the water molecules are always the same. They are simply affected differently by the environment.

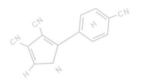

A liquid is defined by the shape of its container.

HOW WE KNOW

What are Elements?

Elements are substances made up entirely of one type of atom. There are 113 different elements, but only 92 occur naturally on Earth. The other elements have to be synthesized, or made, by chemists. Elements are organized according to the Periodic Table of the Elements. This table helps chemists understand why chemicals behave as they do in various states.

Scientific Method

The scientific method is a way of examining the world, running experiments, and building science-based knowledge. By figuring out how things work, scientists are able to use the scientific method to develop new knowledge about the world.

Stepping in the Method

The scientific method is a process that scientists follow in conducting science-based experiments. The process ensures that science is **objective**, based on fact, and that other scientists can understand and repeat the experiments. Here is a set of steps for the scientific method:

1) Ask a question.

2) Read and research what is already known about your question.

3) Come up with a hypothesis (an educated guess about what is happening).

4) Generate an experiment that tests your hypothesis.

5) Run your experiment.

6) Record your observations and results.

7) Analyze your results.

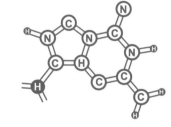

Scientists Ask Why?

A large part of being a scientist consists of asking, "Why?" In seeking to understand how the world works, scientists have to question assumptions, or general beliefs. Scientists might have asked some of the same questions that you have asked, such as: "Why do I have to use toothpaste?" Or "Why does cough syrup taste so bad?" Or "How does a Band-Aid work?" We can find answers from our parents, or teachers, or in books like this one. Knowledge is available, and searching and finding it allows you to understand why things happen. From this base of knowledge, you can create a hypothesis, or an educated explanation for why things happen. A hypothesis is like a temporary answer. When scientists create experiments to test hypotheses, they are trying to figure out whether the answer is true or false. By looking at the results of experiments, scientists can determine if their hypotheses, or educated guesses, are actually true. Hypotheses are often wrong, but they serve a very important purpose in science.

Looking at the results of an experiment can help a scientist confirm whether their hypothesis was correct.

What is an Observation?

Imagine that you had to identify three different common medicine cabinet items with your eyes closed. Could you tell the difference between toothpaste and hand lotion on your finger with your eyes closed? How would you pick out the differences? When you notice the differences between items like these, you are making observations. Making observations of your environment is part of science. When scientists make observations, they record, measure, or write down what they sense. Scientists will often use instruments to help make observations because the things they are trying to observe are often too difficult for human senses to measure accurately. Observations are essential to chemistry.

Hypothesis

Have you ever imagined that you could fly? Doing so creates a hypothetical situation. When you imagine, you use your mind to create a scenario where you can fly. Scientists use hypotheses all the time in their work. A hypothesis is an educated guess or prediction about how particular phenomena occur. By using accurate hypotheses, chemists are able to develop experiments that test what they think is true. Scientists don't always guess correctly though. Sometimes, they can make mistakes and end up misunderstanding what is actually happening. Even mistakes are useful because scientists can use their incorrect hypotheses to make better predictions in the future.

Measuring and recording is important in science.

Theory and Law

Scientific laws are the rules that determine how matter acts in particular environments. A scientific law is a general truth about how things function and is accepted by the majority of scientists. Laws are held to be true until they can no longer provide explanations for observed phenomena. Scientists use theories as models that explain particular behaviors or actions in matter that do not fit into laws. Theories are general ideas of how things operate that have not been completely proven. Through experimentation and analysis, some theories develop into laws. Many scientific laws were once theories that few people in the world believed. For example, for a long period of time people believed Earth was the center of the universe. Through experimentation, observation, and calculation, astronomers demonstrated that Earth orbited the Sun.

Analysis assists scientists in understanding what has happened in experiments.

HOW WE KNOW

The Chemistry of Toothpaste

Several times a day, we brush our teeth using toothpaste. Have you ever wondered what was in toothpaste? Each toothpaste brand is different, but they generally all have common ingredients. Fluoride is essential to cavity prevention. Fluoride comes from fluorine, an extremely poisonous and volatile gas. Toothpaste also contains detergents that foam when you brush. Unfortunately, detergents taste really, really bad. So, toothpaste also has artificial sweeteners and flavors added to hide that taste. So, when you next open your toothpaste tube, remember you are opening a container of highly complex chemicals.

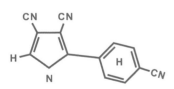

Everyday Chemistry

The medicine cabinet stores a lot of products created through the miracle of chemistry. Even small things such as common pain relievers are made from chemical substances that took years of research to develop. When you next peek into the medicine cabinet, remember how much chemistry is contained behind its door.

Toothpaste foams in your mouth because of the chemical reaction between a detergent and water and your act of brushing or agitating.

In the Cabinet

When you look into a medicine cabinet, think about how much chemistry is involved in the products stored there. On the package of a tube of toothpaste for example, there is a list of both medicinal ingredients and non-medicinal ingredients that combine in a chemical compound. Medicinal ingredients are ones that accomplish the goal of a medicine. For example, in toothpaste, sodium fluoride is a common medicinal ingredient. Non-medicinal ingredients are ones that are in products, but do not accomplish the primary goal. For example, in toothpaste, sodium lauryl sulphate is a detergent that causes it to foam. This foaming action prevents the toothpaste from dripping down your chin, but it doesn't actually clean your teeth.

Talc is the world's softest known substance. It is a mineral powder used in industry and in cosmetics.

Polish Remover as a Solvent

Nail polish remover is a smelly, powerful chemical solution made primarily of the chemical acetone. When you remove nail polish from toenails, acetone acts as a solvent. A solvent is a chemical substance that dissolves another substance or compound into itself. The acetone dissolves the nail polish and turns it into a liquid again. Once the polish is liquid, it can be easily wiped off. But why does this happen? The key is that bottled nail polish contains a very small amount of acetone that prevents it from hardening inside the bottle. When polish is applied, it begins to dry. This drying process occurs as the acetone evaporates, leaving the hardened polish residue behind. Nail polish will not wash off with water, soap, or other detergents because these liquids are not solvents for the polish.

Nail polish remover is an everyday solvent.

Medicine Cabinet Lab

The connection between chemistry and the contents of a medicine cabinet is plain to see. Chemists are employed in the pharmaceutical industry creating life-saving medications. **Antibiotics**, painkillers, cough and cold **suppressants**, and other medications have all been invented by chemists and other scientists. Chemists must ensure that medications work properly. When you consider all of the different types of medications available (both prescription and over-the-counter) and the number of chemists employed in research and development, as well as manufacturing, it is truly astronomical. And that is just medicine. The lotions, makeup, toothpaste, sunscreens, shaving creams, razors, and perfumes in your medicine cabinet have all been developed by chemists.

Chemists were involved in making these drugs.

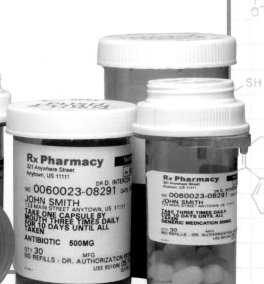

In the Medicine Cabinet

Have you ever wondered how many of the everyday items in your family's medicine cabinet work? What makes baby shampoo so mild? How does aspirin relieve a headache? The answers lie in chemistry!

Ouch! Rip it Off!

Adhesive bandages are handy inventions that allow scrapes and sores to be covered without a bulky wrap. Adhesive bandages are a product of modern chemistry that did not exist until the early 1900s! The outside of a simple bandage is a complex plastic **polymer** that is flexible and strong, while still allowing air circulation. It sticks through an adhesive that is also plastic, but in liquid form, allowing it to stick to the skin and create a seal. The gauze, which is a blend of plastics and organic material such as cotton, pulls blood from the wound and allows the bandage to act as a temporary scab until real healing begins.

The Band-Aid brand of adhesive bandages was invented in 1920 by a Johnson & Johnson employee.

Hydrogen Peroxide

Hydrogen peroxide, or H_2O_2, is a very common medicine cabinet item largely because it can be used in a number of different ways. Peroxide works as a **disinfectant** and an **antiseptic**. Peroxide is used to clean small wounds and prevent infection. It can even remove **pollutants** from wastewater. When poured onto a cut, peroxide bubbles white foam. These are oxygen bubbles that are released from peroxide interacting with catalase, an enzyme found in blood. As many blondes know, peroxide also works as a common bleaching agent used to either dye or create highlights in hair. By applying peroxide, the shaft of the hair is opened and the hair color inside (melanin) is stripped away, causing the hair to lighten or bleach.

Peroxide can bleach hair by stripping away color.

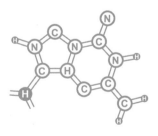

fun fact

Some toothpastes have antimicrobial chemicals that kill some of the tiny microorganisms in your mouth that cause bad breath and disease.

Vitamins Before Dinner

Many families keep vitamins in their medicine cabinets. Whether a multivitamin made up of a daily dose of a large number of vitamins and minerals, or pure vitamin C, vitamins are made through chemical processes. The vitamins that you take are made through refining, processing, and **distilling** various substances down to the vitamins in their pure form. These pure vitamins are then mixed to the proper quantity in other substances to make the physical vitamin that you swallow. The key to having essential vitamins for your body is eating a healthy and varied diet.

Making vitamins is a time-consuming process that requires a knowledge of chemistry.

HOW WE KNOW

Safety and the Medicine Cabinet

When we deal with some chemicals, there is an element of danger. Some items found in the medicine cabinet have the potential to be very harmful. Both over-the-counter and prescription medications found in the medicine cabinet can be extremely harmful. Even simple items like nail polish remover or peroxide are toxic if handled improperly. Whenever you need to get something out of the medicine cabinet, always ask a parent for help. The best way to avoid danger is knowing where it exists.

Prescription Medicines

When we are really sick, we go to the doctor's office. Depending on what we have, our doctor may prescribe a medication to help lessen the symptoms of the illness or cure it. When a doctor prescribes a medication, this means you are allowed to use a chemical that is not ordinarily available. Prescription medicines range from antibiotics used to fight bacterial infections to medications that lower blood pressure to extra strength painkillers. Some prescription medications are for short-term use like antibiotics, while others like insulin, which is used to treat diabetes, are lifelong medications. The development of prescription medicines takes a long time and a lot of money for pharmaceutical companies. The people who develop drugs are often biochemists who understand how certain chemical compounds work in the body. A drug may be in development for over 15 years before it can be sold on the market. Even then, it is made and sold under strick conditions.

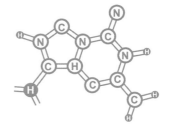

Drugs are made under strict conditions. This "clean room" at a pharmaceutical plant is so sterile that the people who mix ingredients wear protective suits over their clothing so nothing contaminates the drugs.

Testing Theories

Chemistry is all about experimentation. One of the joys of doing chemistry is that it allows you to discover and understand how and why matter works.

Experiments

Humans experiment all the time. Young children experiment with walking and talking until they become good at these skills. Scientists experiment in much the same way. Through trial and error, scientists develop experiments that provide results that prove or disprove a hypothesis. Through observing and recording the results of an experiment, scientists are able to advance knowledge in their field.

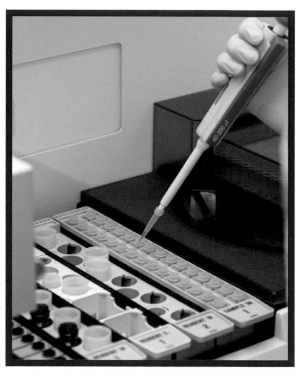

Chemists (above and below) test, observe, and analyze in a pharmaceutical laboratory.

Testing and Observing

Testing is an important part of scientific experimentation. By running experiments several times, scientists can provide evidence that shows whether particular theories and hypotheses are true. When scientists test through experimentation, they need to carefully observe and record the results. With sound results, they can provide strong evidence that their model or representation of particular phenomena is accurate. Scientists will often use tools to aid in observation such as telescopes for viewing the stars, or microscopes for viewing tiny structures like atoms.

Measuring the Results

How tall are you? Your height is a measurement. Scientists use measurements to show the results of their experiments. When results are measured, it is possible to compare them and understand them better. Measurements can determine mass, or how much something weighs, length, or how long something is, temperature, or how hot or cold something is, or various other properties. Scientists measure volume, temperature, mass, and the type of compounds produced through a chemical reaction.

Analysis

What do scientists do once they have a set of results? First, they look for patterns that fit their hypotheses. It is the scientist's job to solve the puzzle by putting the pieces from the experiment and their scientific understanding together. If the analysis does not prove the hypothesis, scientists need to know why and how to change it to demonstrate the hypothesis more clearly. Sometimes, scientists will realize through analyzing their data that they are on the wrong track. When this happens, they have to rethink their whole hypotheses and process of experimentation.

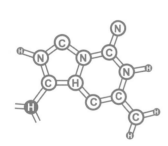

In laboratories, chemists use equipment such as microscopes to help them observe experiments.

Fizzy Reaction

What makes a product fizz and bubble?

Question: Can simple ingredients have the same results as a commercial indigestion reliever?

Hypothesis: Effervescence can be created through a simple baking soda reaction.

Materials:

1 tablet of an antacid reliever
1 tablespoon (15 ml) baking soda
1 tablespoon (15 ml) citric acid or calcium citrate (found in drug stores)
2 glasses
measuring cup and spoons
tap water

Method:

1. Fill one large glass with about 1 cup (250 ml) of water.
2. Put a tablespoon of citric acid and baking soda in another glass of the same size (without water). Note: If the citric acid is in pill form (such as calcium citrate), crush the pills, remove the shells, and measure the powder.
3. Drop the antacid in the glass with the water. Make observations.
4. Pour 1 cup (250 ml) of water in the glass with the baking soda mixture. Make observations.
5. Compare the observations of each reaction.

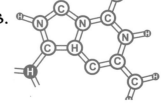

Pour water in one glass and put the baking soda and citric acid in the other.

Drop the antacid into the glass with the water and observe.

Mix the baking soda and citric acid with water and observe.

Are there slight differences in reactions?

Results and Discussion:

The chemical reaction causes rapid bubbling because baking soda (sodium bicarbonate) is a base and the citric acid is an acid. The bubbles you observe are carbon dioxide.

Why would an alkali-based mixture (the commercial antacid) aid with indigestion and stomach upset? Remember that your stomach breaks down food using strong acids.

*Warning: Do not drink either experiment. Commercial antacids contain aspirin and can be harmful if swallowed.

Balloon Blowout

We can't see carbon dioxide but we can prove it exists.

Question: What can a simple, safe reaction tell us about states of matter?

Hypothesis: Baking soda and vinegar can create a chemical reaction that changes a liquid to a gas.

Materials:

Empty, clean plastic soda bottle
1 balloon
1/4 cup white vinegar
1/3 cup baking soda
spoons

Method:

1. Carefully fill a balloon with baking soda.
2. Pour vinegar into the clean soda bottle.
3. Carefully stretch the balloon over the mouth of the bottle.
4. Let the baking soda settle from the balloon into the bottle containing the vinegar.

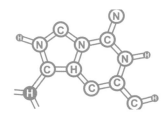

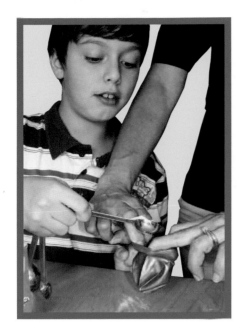

Fill the balloon with baking soda.

Add the vinegar into the bottle.

Place the balloon filled with baking soda over the bottle's mouth.

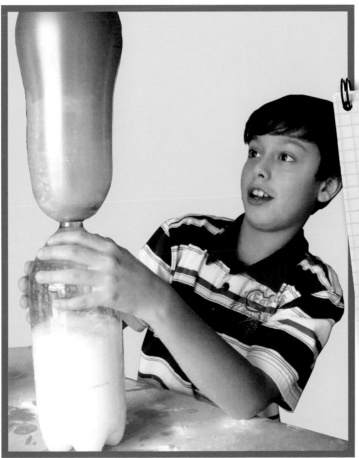

Kablamie! Observe how the reaction looks and feels.

Results and Discussion:

Baking soda is a chemical called sodium bicarbonate. When mixed with vinegar it reacts to form a gas. You can see this from the way the balloon inflated when the reaction took place. The baking soda mixture may have also quickly fizzed and bubbled.

The gas created from this change of state is carbon dioxide. It filled the balloon and caused it to expand. Did the bottle feel a little cold after the reaction? This is called an endothermic reaction because it uses heat to help fuel the reaction.

Eureka! I Found It!

"Eureka!" screamed Archimedes after realizing that the volume of water displaced in his bathtub was equal to the volume of his body. In Greek, eureka means "I have found it."

Lucky Accident

Ancient Greek scientist Archimedes came upon his lucky discovery while bathing! It helped him solve a difficult scientific problem of how to measure the volume of something. The history of science is a history of lucky accidents where scientists set out to prove one thing and end up with something entirely different. If they weren't clever and observant like Archimedes, most would not even be able to see that their lucky accidents were really incredible discoveries.

Ever since Archimedes, people have used the term "eureka" to proclaim a discovery or a sudden understanding of a problem.

Seaweed to Disinfectant

Iodine, a mild disinfectant and antiseptic used to treat cuts and wounds, was accidentally discovered by French chemist Bernard Courtois in 1811. Courtois owned a company that made saltpeter, an ingredient in gunpowder made from the ashes of burned seaweed. One day he added too much sulphuric acid to his ashes. Instead of the saltpeter ingredient, there was a large explosion followed by a purplish vapor. After further experiments by chemists, this vapor was **isolated** and named iodine. Iodine has many uses, including cleaning wounds and swabbing stitches, purifying water, and given in medicine for X-rays.

Iodine was an accidental discovery now used around the world to disinfect prior to surgery. The yellow stain is iodine.

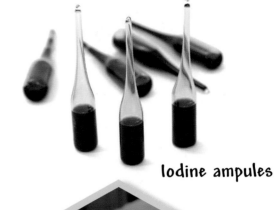

Iodine ampules

HOW WE KNOW

The Natural World as a Drugstore

The plant kingdom is the world's largest drugstore. Many of the world's potent pharmaceuticals come from plants. Opiates are a class of drugs derived from the opium poppy plant. They include morphine, codeine, thebaine, and papaverine, all strong painkillers. Taxol, a cancer drug used to treat tumors, comes from the Pacific Yew tree. Chemists isolated and synthesized the drugs from the original plants, and over time, after learning their chemical makeup, discovered how to replicate, or copy their effects using other substances such as petrochemicals.

Quinine and Malaria

Quinine, a malaria treatment, was first used by the Quechua Indians of Peru to stop their muscles from shaking and shivering as an affect of the disease. The Indians would chew on the bark of the quina or cinchona tree and their muscles would relax. In the 1600s, malaria was common in Italy and especially in the marshes that surrounded Rome. An Italian priest who lived in Peru saw how the Indians used the bark. The priest had trained as a **pharmacist** and noticed how the shaking disappeared when the bark was chewed. He sent a shipment of the bark to Rome to treat malaria. Quinine, the active ingredient in the bark, was isolated by chemists in the 1700s, and later produced as a drug. Quinine saved many lives. Small quantities of quinine can be found in tonic water, a carbonated beverage with a bitter taste. The alcoholic drink gin and tonic has its beginnings in India where British **colonials** mixed the quinine they used to fight malaria, with gin to disguise the bitter taste of quinine.

Malaria is spread by infected mosquitoes. Quinine was the first medicine that fought the effects of the disease.

fun fact

"The important thing in science is not so much to obtain new facts as to discover new ways of thinking about them" –William Lawrence Bragg, Nobel Prize winning physicist

Accidental Pain Reliever

Tylenol is the name brand for a series of painkilling and fever-reducing drugs that contain acetaminophen, or paracetamol. Acetaminophen's medical properties were discovered through a strange twist. Two French doctors ordered a common drug called naphthalene to help fight infections in their patients. Through a mistaken delivery, they received a relatively unknown drug called acetanilide, which was advertised as a painkiller. They gave this medication to their patients and discovered both the pain-killing and fever-reducing abilities. Unfortunately, the medication remained obscure until the 1950s when the more common painkiller Aspirin, or acetylsalicylic acid, was linked to Reye's syndrome, an often fatal disease in children. Tylenol is the number one analgesic, or painkiller, and has annual sales of over $1 billion.

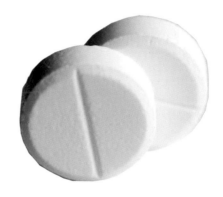

Acetaminophen's pain-killing and fever-reducing properties were discovered by accident.

HOW WE KNOW

Elixer Chemtastrophe

In 1937, a new drug designed to fight germs called Elixir Sulfanilamide was released in the United States. The elixir caused a mass poisoning where over 100 patients who had used the elixir died. At the time there were no regulations ensuring medicines were safe. The U.S. government quickly passed a set of laws called the 1938 Federal Food, Drug and Cosmetic Act. This act required pharmaceutical companies to label all medical ingredients, and test the safety of drugs and other products for human **consumption**.

Creative Chemists

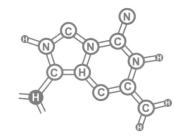

Chemists work in a wide variety of jobs depending on their area of specialization. Chemists are employed in the pharmaceutical industry both in research and manufacturing.

Awesome Chemistry

Chemists can create new molecules and compounds, analyze and synthesize various substances, and predict how certain substances will interact in ways that would seem like magic to people 100 years ago. The rate of advancement in chemistry is incredible. Many of the products in our medicine cabinets are inventions of the last 50 years. Just imagine what chemists will be able to do in the next 100 years. Perhaps there will be self-brushing toothpaste!

Imagine how much worse illnesses would be if there were no drugs to fight them.

Research and Development

The pharmaceutical industry develops and produces drugs and medications and has a specific area called research and development. The chemists involved in research and development attempt to create molecules, compounds, and other drugs to treat, heal, and cure many illnesses and diseases. Research and development costs are very high. It costs on average between $50 and $70 million dollars to produce just one type of drug—and that's before testing on humans. That's a lot of money for a drug that may never be sold. Of the molecules developed, approximately 18 percent get approval from the government for sale to humans.

Drug companies use sophisticated and expensive equipment to produce products.

fun fact

"Basic research is like shooting an arrow into the air and, where it lands, painting a target."
-Homer Burtun Adkins, organic chemist

Want to Learn More?

Do you want to become a pharmacist or find out how drugs and other medicines that help us are made? Here are some fantastic sources to use when learning about medicine cabinet chemistry.

Chemistry Websites:

Rader's Chem4Kids!
www.chem4kids.com
A fascinating website that offers an introductory perspective on chemical concepts such as atoms, molecules, reactions, and much more. Games and quizzes are also available on the site.

Strange Matter
www.strangematterexhibit.com/index.html
An exciting and interactive website that looks at chemical concepts through material science. With both educational videos and fun games, there is something for everyone here.

Try Science
www.tryscience.org/home.html
Learn trivia, find cool experiments to do at home, and watch live video of scientific projects on this kid-central website.

Science Made Simple
www.sciencemadesimple.com/
Get some great ideas for your next science project, and find fun chemistry activities you can do at home or with your friends and family.

BrainPop
www.brainpop.com/science/matterandchemistry/
Find answers to all your chemistry questions!

Chemistry Books:

Why Chemistry Matters series. Crabtree Publishing, 2009. This series uses common examples from everyday life to help explain basic chemistry.

Health And Medicine (Science News for Kids) by Tara Koellhoffer: Chelsea Clubhouse, 2006. This detailed and interesting book focuses on some of the latest developments in science and medicine.

Chemistry by Dr. Anne Newmark: Dorling Kindersley, 2000. This book has ample and varied information on topics in chemistry.

The Sky's the Limit: Stories of Discovery by Women and Girls by Catherine Thimmesh and Melissa Sweet: Sandpiper, 2004. Be inspired by the contributions that women have made to our understanding of science.

Step into Science series. Crabtree Publishing, 2010. Each book in this series explores a step in the scientific method.

Places to Learn More:

Howard Hughes Medical Institute
Chevy Chase, Maryland
This research and education institute offers summer science and medicine-based programming through their GreenKids Project and Cool Science initiative.

Lawrence Hall of Science
Berkeley, California
This research museum offers full programming for K–12 students with interactive exhibits and science camps.

Smithsonian National Museum of Natural History
Washington, DC
The Smithsonian is a dynamic educational environment for children and adults alike. Learn about all aspects of science while exploring the interactive exhibits.

Glossary

antibiotics Drugs used to destroy or prevent the growth of bacteria or other disease-causing organisms

antiseptic A substance or drug that kills germs that cause disease or decay

colonials People who settle in a territory controlled by a distant country

compounds A mixture or something made up of two or more parts or elements

condenses To change from a gas to a liquid or solid

conducted To carry or allow passage through or along

consumption The act or process of using up or consuming something

disinfectant Something that kills germs

distilling The process of heating a substance to produce a vapor, which is then cooled and condensed, in order to purify, concentrate, or extract components from the substance

fluoride A chemical compound that contains fluorine as one of its elements

isolated To extract something in a pure form

nucleus The central, essential, or most active part around which other parts are grouped

objective An aim, goal, or purpose that a person works to achieve

pharmacist A person who is trained to prepare and sell drugs and medicine ordered through a doctor

pollutants Something that pollutes, or contaminates, such as a waste substance that makes air, water, or land impure or unhealthy

polymer A natural or synthetic compound, such as polyethylene or nylon, that is of high molecular weight and is composed of repeated links of simple molecules

properties A quality that something is known by; characteristic

suppressants A drug designed to prevent undesirable symptoms or conditions

Index